I dedicate this book to my loving wife, Judith Ann Lauber – Judi with an "i".

She left me way too soon but truly made my life complete.

I also dedicate it to our four amazing daughters, our 10 awesome grandchildren,

and those who are yet to come.

I love you all.

Text copyright © 2022 by James Lauber
Photo credits: James Lauber
Published by The Wordly Group
Printed in the U.S.A.
First Printing, 2022
ISBN: 978-1-7350221-9-2

The Wordly Group
www.thewordlygroup.com

MY LIFE AS I REMEMBER IT

The Memoirs of James Michael Lauber

Lois Lindsey Hito

CONTENTS

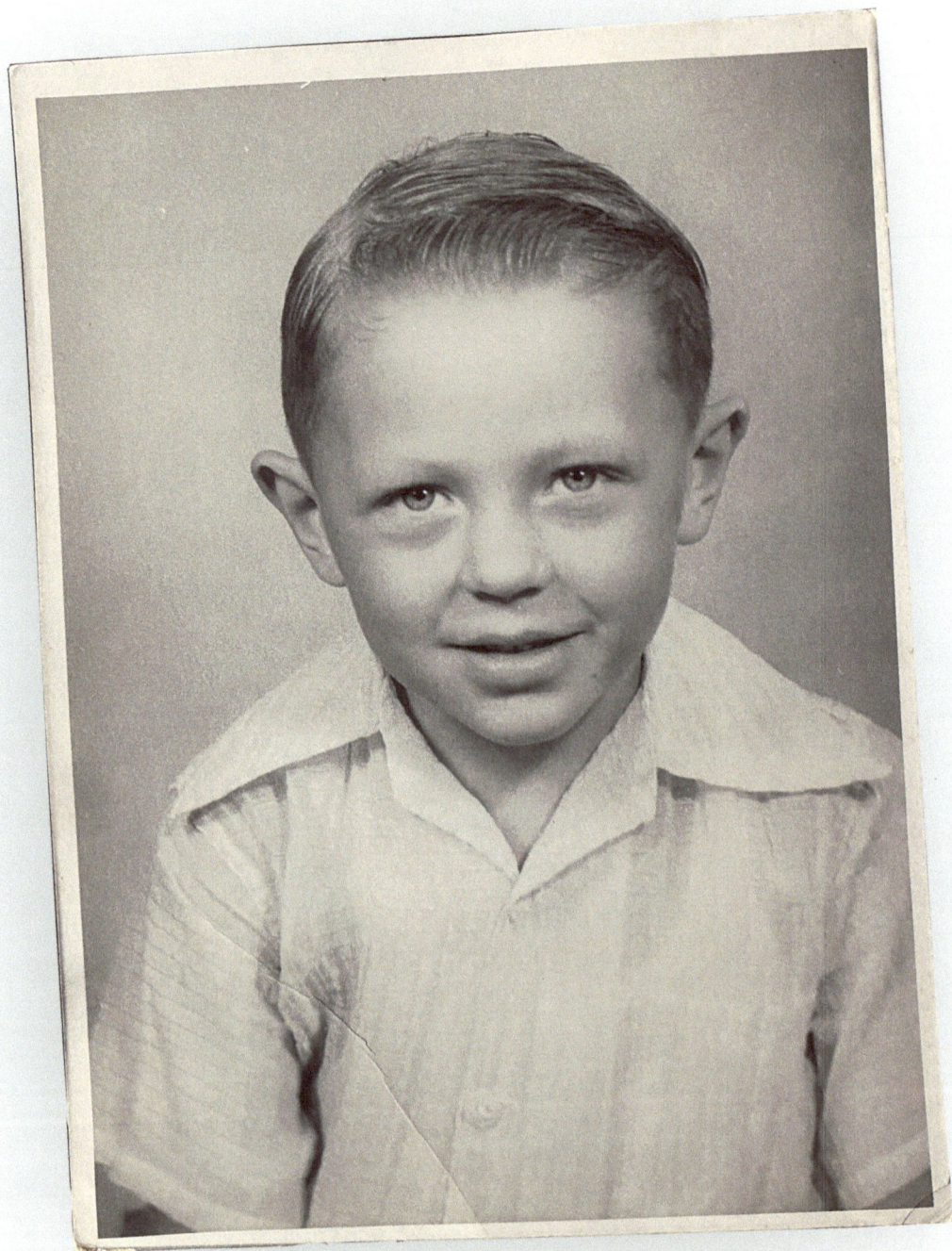

AN INTRODUCTION

I have decided to record these memories for two reasons. First, I was prompted by a number of family members to do so. And second, I often wish I had a picture, a glimpse, into the lives of my own ancestors. I want to provide that for my descendants.

I am not a scholarly person – writing is not one of the skills I've cultivated, so please bear with me. This is as much a book of pictures as it is a book of words. As they say, a picture is worth a thousand words.

I regret that in this book I do not share more about my parents, grandparents, brothers, sisters, nieces, nephews, and friends – and especially my wonderful daughters and grandchildren. God has truly blessed me with an amazing family and group of friends. But this memoir is about me and the memories I have created throughout my life. Hopefully, in the future, my children and grandchildren will add to it. This is only a snapshot. There is much more that I could have included, but it may never have ended. Recording these memories has led me to many smiles and many tears, and it has been gratifying and therapeutic to relive my life throughout this process.

The time of this writing is the year 2022. I am in my 74th year.

This is a picture postcard of our farm in 1919 that my grandfather sent to my grandmother before they were married.

This is what we managed to decipher from the back:

February 13, 1919
Miss Syrena Clauer
Oakwood, Wisconsin

Hello Kid,
Well how is Syrena? I'm fine. Was going to write a letter but have no paper so you must excuse . . . for this time. Say kid I had some fine time getting home Sunday night as I got out on the road. I thought I had a flat tire so I went out and . . . enough to get on . . . so it was 3 o'clock as I got home, some weather, we got to . . . Will write . . . next time . . . O.K. see you Sat. . . . Albert . . .

My parents, Clarence and Leora Lauber (née Blomberg), were the most loving, selfless Christian parents a child could have.

My parents, Clarence and Leora Lauber (née Blomberg)

My paternal grandparents were Alfred and Francis Lauber. They were dairy farmers and lived on a farm in Union Grove, Wisconsin, which was 15 miles south of the farm we lived on growing up. They had six children – two boys and four girls.

My maternal grandparents were Albert and Syrena Blomberg. They were also dairy farmers, and they lived on our family farm in Franklin, Wisconsin. They had two children, both girls.

Alfred and Francis Lauber (née Wendt)

Albert and Syrena Blomberg (née Clauer)

All four of my grandparents were good Christian people. The Lauber and Blomberg families were first-generation Americans of German descent. All were members of the Wisconsin Evangelical Lutheran Synod, and they lived lives that I can only pray to emulate.

In addition to my parents and grandparents, I have five siblings – two brothers and three sisters. Growing up, the six of us had six aunts, six uncles, and 26 cousins. We were a large, very close, and loving family, which was such a blessing. My mom and dad were incredibly fine, selfless Christian parents.

MY CHILDHOOD

I was born on September 2, 1947. At the time of my birth, we lived on a small farm in the Town of Franklin, which later became the City of Franklin.

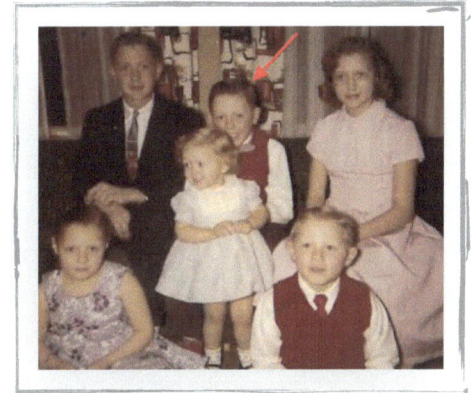

My earliest memory of childhood was being in a walker watching my grandpa installing ceiling tiles on the farmhouse ceiling. Since I would have been younger than a year old, it could very well be nothing more than a figment of my imagination. But it's a vivid memory that I've always had.

I was blessed to have grown up with wonderful siblings – my two brothers, Dave and Keith, and my three sisters, Kathleen, Karen, and Nancy. We filled an entire pew at church.

We three boys shared a small bedroom that had no closet, the three girls shared another small bedroom, and the bedrooms had a door that connected them. It was perhaps cramped by today's standards, but I remember it being more of a blessing than a hardship.

We would talk together before going to sleep, and sometimes we boys would sneak into the girls' room and try to scare them. I remember standing in a dark closet for long periods of time, just waiting for one of the girls to open the door so I could scare the bejeebers out of them. We would say our bedtime prayers and finally go to sleep. When someone started talking in their sleep, we would try to carry on a conversation with them, and it actually worked.

I remember my parents square dancing and my dad playing horseshoes in a league that he and his friends from church had formed. Both of my parents were active at our church, serving on various boards and organizations.

I remember my dad being a hardworking man who worked all day at the company Ladish, farmed part-time, and still made time to play catch with us. He would always slip me a few bucks and give me a ride when I wanted to go skating or to a movie with my friends.

I remember my mother taking us to the beach so we could go swimming in the summer. She was a great cook and baker, and she looked after our every need. She loved big snowstorms and when we were all snowed in together. During our teenage years, she wouldn't go to sleep until we were all home safe and sound. She knew exactly what time each of our cars pulled into the driveway.

I thought my mother was prettiest when she was pregnant. I have two more brothers – one was stillborn and one was a miscarriage. I remember my mother and my oldest sister being pregnant at the same time. Had my mother not lost the baby, I would have had a younger brother and a nephew the same age.

Growing up on a small farm with brothers, sisters, and neighbor kids made for an absolutely wonderful childhood. And having loving Christian grandparents living right upstairs was an added blessing.

There was a row of lush purple and white lilac bushes at the end of our driveway. Coming up it – driving on the crushed limestone that was stained purple from the smashed fruit from the mulberry tree – you passed our big white farmhouse, trimmed in green with a bridal wreath bush by the front porch and morning glories climbing up the side of the back porch. Entering the yard, there was the big red barn, trimmed in white with the year it was built – 1907 – painted on its side. This number is special to all of us. It's one we will never forget and that most of us still use to this day for our garage door codes, phone numbers, or passwords.

The barn and house were surrounded by almost two acres of lush, well-manicured grass dotted with bright yellow dandelions. There was a machine shed – a brooder house – where every year we would raise about 250 baby chickens. There was a 300-gallon red gas tank for filling the tractors, a rusty old burning barrel where we would burn our garbage, a smokehouse for smoking ham and bacon, an old outhouse for . . . well, you know what for . . . and a summer kitchen where, before my time, the cooking would be done in the summer, so you wouldn't heat up the house.

On the lawn were 15-foot-high swings. They were the best swings ever. There was also a slide that we would slide down while sitting on wax paper for lubrication, a dollhouse we could play in next to a large sandbox, a picnic table, horseshoe pits, and a large garden filled with all kinds of vegetables, strawberries, raspberries, and even some weeds. There were many shade trees, a horse chestnut tree, an apple tree, a Bartlett pear tree

Lauber family farm – 1981

that produced delicious pears, and a white flowering crab tree that burst into beautiful white blossoms every year for Mother's Day. My grandpa told me that the pear tree was grafted with an apple tree and would produce both pears and apples.

We basically had our own park and playground. There was no end to the adventures and things to do, even without the aid of electronics, television, or sports clubs. The phrase "we're bored" was never a part of our vocabulary. When we got up in the morning, after breakfast, outside we went as fast as we could. If it was summer, we ran around barefoot, running across the gravel driveway and hay stubble fields. Except for meals, we didn't come back in the house until our parents made us come in for bed.

I remember building hay forts with tunnels in the hay mow, walking the barn beams, catching pigeons by hand, riding our bikes down the barn hill and launching off a homemade ramp, riding cows and pigs, playing "Cowboys and Indians" with real bows and arrows and BB guns, having rotten-duck-egg fights, and fishing at the Root River. Occasionally, a prisoner from the prison farm nearby asked to borrow some worms or a hook and line. I remember ice skating on the pond at the City Farm, which was right across the street, where they grew all the trees for the City of Milwaukee. We rented and farmed whatever wasn't planted with trees; they paid us a dollar to make it legal. Every fall when my mother was a young girl, the city would bring in reindeer, and an Eskimo would train them to pull the sleigh for the City of Milwaukee's Christmas parade.

Life on a farm was a lot of work. As kids, though, we didn't have to do a lot – just enough to help build our character and work ethic. We would pick rocks from the fields, pull mustard plants and hoe thistles in the grain fields, and bale and unload hay. Riding home from the field on top of a wagon loaded high with bales was a great feeling. When we unloaded the hay up in the hay mow and got to that last bale on the wagon, my dad would shout, "There's the one we were looking for." When he did that, it was time for him to run the wagon down the barn hill by hand. By the time it got to the bottom of the hill, it seemed as if it was going 100 miles an hour. It was quite the sight. When we were all done – hot, sweaty, and covered in hay chaff – we would run down to the milk house and get a drink of ice cold water from the jug that was kept in the milk cooler. Water never tasted so good. Finally, we would jump in our above-ground pool to cool off.

Then, there were the animals. We had cows, pigs, chickens, ducks, geese, and an occasional goat or sheep. There was always a dog and a multitude of barn cats. We even had pet raccoons and skunks, which my older brother Dave caught and had deodorized. There were large flocks of wild pheasants running everywhere. Today, there are no longer pheasants in that area.

I remember helping a neighbor with his farm work. With the money I earned working for him, I bought my first horse from him, a big old paint named Lucky. It was a dream come true for me. I rode him with such pride. When the Franklin high school – which I soon would be attending – was being built next to our farm, I would ride Lucky up and down the hallways on the weekends, when nobody was there. It was a fond memory I carried throughout my high school years.

I remember being kicked by cows, thrown off my horse, chased by geese, zapped by the electric fence, stepping on rusty nails, and getting slivers by the hundreds. Tetanus shots, Mercurochrome that stung like heck, tweezers, and drawing salve were the norm.

To this day, I can still recall the sounds of farm life – the call of a killdeer protecting her chicks; the crow of pheasants in the fields; the sounds of cows bellowing, horses neighing, pigs grunting, sheep bleating, roosters crowing, geese hissing, and baby chicks peeping; the sound of the haybaler making hay; and even the sound of our church bell, tolling the age of a member who had died.

The air was filled with smells too. I remember walking into the barn when it was filled with the aroma of fresh hay and cows, smelling the fragrance of freshly cut alfalfa hay and newly plowed ground, enjoying the sweet smell of ground animal feed with molasses mixed in, taking in the fresh smell in the air after a thunderstorm, and, yes, even enduring the smell of the manure pile. The house was filled with the aroma of freshly baked bread, cakes, tortes, pies, and cinnamon rolls. When my mother baked bread, she would save some of the dough and fry it in a cast-iron frying pan. We would smother it with our own homemade butter and strawberry preserves. It was to die for.

Food on the farm was abundant, good, and nutritious. There was fried homemade liver sausage and punic. I've never found anyone who has heard of punic. It was made from the water we boiled pigs' heads in to make the liver sausage, mixed with buckwheat flour, put into a loaf pan, and then thinly sliced and fried for breakfast. Nothing went to waste on the farm. We had a large canning cabinet in the basement, filled with every kind of pickle you can imagine. We canned dilly beans, peaches and pears, tomatoes and tomato juice, beets, and corn relish. Anything that could be canned, we canned it. There were three freezers filled with a side of beef, pork, chicken, duck, goose, sweet corn, and green beans. We could live all winter on what we raised, froze, and canned. Grocery shopping was only for necessities that we were unable to produce ourselves.

On Sundays after church, we would pick up hot ham and hard rolls for lunch – a Milwaukee tradition. Every now and then, we would go to American Soda Water, where we could buy a case and fill it with whatever flavors we wanted – fruit punch, orange, pineapple, and even chocolate and licorice. Going out to eat at a restaurant or for fast food was nearly nonexistent.

For a treat, my dad would pop popcorn, drench it in butter, and make chocolate malts in a hand shaker. My mother had more recipes for snacks and appetizers than you could count. As kids, we had no idea that we were poor. One thing for sure was that we never went hungry.

We got the measles, mumps, and chicken pox. When we had colds and coughs, my mother would rub Vicks VapoRub on our chest and then cover it with a flannel cloth that she had warmed in the oven. She would make hot milk with butter and vanilla in it and tuck us into a warm, heavy quilt. If we had a sore throat, she would have us gargle with salt water.

In school we would get vaccination shots, eye tests, malt tablets, and iodine pills. Polio was a major epidemic when we were young, and we were kept away from having too much contact with the public. After Jonas Salk developed a vaccine for it, we all had to get polio shots. I remember our family going to Dr. Wolf's office for it. When he came out to see us, he said, "Well, the whole fam damily is here."

Going to the dentist was a dreaded experience. Dr. May was a kind older man, but his office was a scary place in my eyes, not to mention sitting in his chair. Drilling was done with a drill powered by a foot pedal.

In those days, services came to you. Doctors made house calls. A fruit-and-vegetable man with a truck loaded full of produce, a grocery truck with an aisle down the center and shelves on both sides loaded with groceries, a Watkins vanilla man, a fuller brush man, a scrap metal and rag man, a juice man with all kinds of juices, and my favorite – an ice cream man – all came to the house. It was our version of Amazon.

We did go to stores to shop, but it was not an everyday occurrence. We would ride our bikes to a small country gas station that was also a penny candy store and buy small wax bottles filled with juice, flying saucers (like a communion wafer filled with beads), wax lips, and just about every candy you could imagine back then.

My parents would shop at Sears on Mitchell Street in Milwaukee. There was a tall tower at the top of the building, and inside that tower was a man who would tell you over a loudspeaker where to park. One car at a time, he would say, for instance, "Gray '56 Chevy station wagon, row three, halfway down." Later, after my wife Judi and I were married, I found out that the man in the tower was her uncle.

I would also go with my grandpa to Winterbergers, a grocery store in downtown Milwaukee that was owned by one of our neighbors. We would deliver cases of eggs and butchered ducks and geese, which he in turn would sell. We also had an egg route, delivering eggs to neighboring subdivisions and bars.

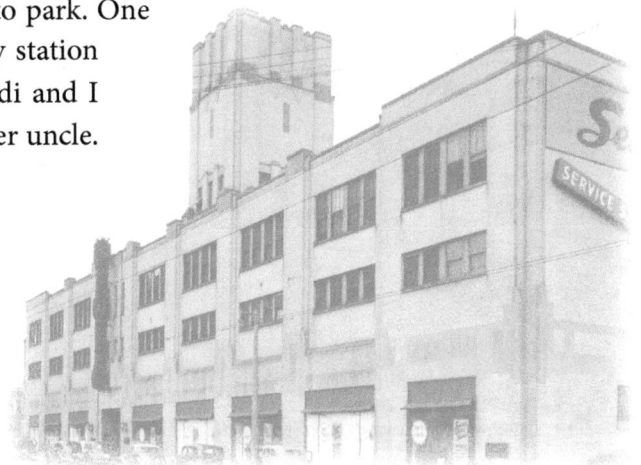

There were birthday parties, anniversary parties, round robins, card parties, weddings, graduations, confirmations, and dinner parties with friends of the family. Every year, my parents invited our teachers and pastors over for supper. Almost every Sunday after church, relatives would stop in for dinner or we would go to their homes for dinner. After dinner, the dishes would be cleared from the table and out came the cards: Sheepshead for the men and women, or sometimes Canasta for the women. As a kid, I was in my glory when my grandma and grandpa would let me be the bartender for their card parties. I would even get tips.

Holidays and parties were abundant. Every year we had large family reunions, one for each side of the family.

Easter was one of my mother's favorite holidays. On Good Friday she would make us prunes and noodles for lunch, a very bland dish meant to signify showing sorrow for our sins. We were always silent between the hours of 12:00 p.m. and 3:00 p.m. These were both German customs, in remembrance of Jesus dying on the cross. She would dye the Easter eggs by boiling them in water with onion shells, making them a dark orange color. Years later, my mother ended up dying on Good Friday, between the hours of 12:00 p.m. and 3:00 p.m.

Christmas was a very busy time of year. It was filled with memorizing and practicing for the Christmas Eve program at church, decorating the church, baking stollen and Christmas cookies of every kind, and making homemade fudge, popcorn balls, and brandy slush. On the way to our Christmas program, my dad always seemed to forget something at home and had to go back after dropping us off at church. He was really just putting the gifts under the tree, because Santa always came while we were at church. The

Christmas Eve service consisted of all the schoolchildren standing up in front singing hymns and reciting the account of Christ's birth. After the service, each of us received a brown paper bag filled with fruit, nuts, and a bit of hard candy. When we returned home, we waited in the kitchen for everybody to arrive before opening the door to the living room, where the tree and gifts were. Then, it was complete chaos opening gifts. My most memorable and meaningful gift was a barn that my dad had built for me.

Christmas Day was celebrated at Grandma and Grandpa Lauber's house with all our aunts, uncles, and cousins – about 50 people in all. During the following week, we would visit every single one of our relatives' homes to see their trees and gifts, and they all came to see ours. We'd have a half-hour visit and one drink at each house, and then we were off to the next house. We usually visited three houses per night, which was a monumental task but so wonderfully family oriented.

Every summer we took a one-week family vacation to various lake cottages in northern Wisconsin, where we would fish, swim, and get to buy a souvenir. At night we would park at the dump and watch the black bears scavenging through the garbage. I remember my mother being trapped in the outhouse because there was a bear between the outhouse and the cottage.

There are just a few more memories that stick out in my mind that I would like to share.

My grandmother told me about two spiritual events that happened during her life, and I have never forgotten them. The first occurred the night her father died. She was very upset and unable to fall asleep. She said that while she was lying awake, an angel sat down next to her on her bed, and from that moment, she felt complete comfort. She felt that comfort throughout the rest of her life, and she never feared death. Near the end, when my mother and her sister were with my grandmother at the hospital, they told her she would be coming home soon. She responded, "It doesn't make any difference to me which home I go to."

The second event happened when my grandmother and several of her sisters were at the bedside of their sister-in-law as she was dying. Stretching her arms out in front of her, she was murmuring, "I can't reach him. I can't reach him. He's right in front of me, but I can't reach him." They kept asking her who was in front of her, who it was that she couldn't reach. After several minutes of this, she finally answered, "Jesus! He's right in front of me, but I can't reach him." Then, with a smile on her face and her arms stretched out, she sighed, "Ah, I've got him." And at that very moment, she died.

While in 4-H, I decided to take up woodworking one year. Shortly after I made that decision, my grandpa dropped me off at school one morning and I slammed the car door with my thumb stuck inside of it. Weeks later, I jumped over a barbed-wire fence, tearing open the tip of my index finger, which required stitches. About a month later, I fell off the pony I was riding and it stepped on my middle finger, tearing it wide open, which required even more stitches. I skipped the next finger, but another month went by and I got my pinky finger caught between a pulley and a v-belt on a well pump, tearing my fingernail off. I injured four out of five fingers in order, all on the same hand, within a two-and-a-half-month period. Needless to say, I was not able to do any woodworking projects that year.

I remember one time one of my neighborhood friends came over to the farm to play. We decided to build a campfire and roast hot dogs for lunch. Halfway through eating, he jumped up with fear on his face and shouted, "It's Friday! I'm Catholic, and I can't eat meat on Fridays! I'm going to hell!" He was scared to death. But we made him a peanut butter and jelly sandwich, told him we wouldn't tell anybody, and all was fine.

We had an older neighbor who, unbeknownst to us, had a glass eye. He would prank us kids by saying, "Oh, my eye is getting dirty." He would then pop it out of the socket and put it in his mouth to clean it off, causing a big bulge in his cheek. You can imagine our shock and the looks on our faces the first time he did it.

One year we used another neighbor's corn picker to pick our corn. When we were done, my dad offered to pick his corn. He declined and said his hired man would do it. The next day his hired man got his arm caught in the picker, tearing it off. He had to crawl a quarter of a mile back to their farm with a severed arm. It was amazing he didn't bleed to death.

MY SCHOOL YEARS

I must confess, school was not my friend. However, attending a Christian grade school was a positive influence that helped form me into who I am today. I went to St. Paul's Lutheran School from kindergarten through eighth grade. It was a small, two-room, old-fashioned country school next to our church and two miles from our farm. The average class size was seven or eight kids.

Our pastor was the principal, and there were two teachers – one for kindergarten through fourth grade and the other for fifth grade through eighth grade. I made many friends there, and many are still friends to this day. Though I never liked school, I did take away many good things from grade school, the most important of which was building on the foundation of my faith that my parents had laid. In addition to reading, writing, and arithmetic, we took confirmation classes and were examined and confirmed when we were in eighth grade.

In addition to schoolwork, we did janitorial work. We cleaned the school, burned the garbage, shoveled snow, cleaned the school and church grounds, and raised and lowered the flag.

We had a baseball field behind the school that was also a cow pasture for a neighbor's cows. We had to climb over a fence to get to it and watch where we stepped to avoid the cow pies and the cows. We also had a basketball team.

I would do anything to get out of going to school. Sometimes I feigned being sick. One time I put the thermometer in a glass of warm water, but for some reason my mother didn't believe I had a 112-degree temperature.

After grade school, I went on to high school. I spent my freshman year at Greendale High School, because Franklin High School was still in the process of being built. My sophomore, junior, and senior years were at the brand-new Franklin High School, the same school where I rode Lucky up and down the hallways.

On the first day of school my Sophomore year, our brand-new principal had an assembly to introduce himself and all the new teachers. He then proceeded to show us a movie that he had taken that summer, since he was new to the area. The film showed the process of the new school being built and the surrounding city of Franklin. All of a sudden, there I was, on the screen, bailing hay. That was my Golden Globe award moment.

Since it was a brand-new school, it started with just freshmen and sophomores. The next year included freshmen, sophomores, and juniors. And the next, freshmen, sophomores, juniors, and seniors. Because of this, we were always the upperclassmen. We got to pick the school song, the school colors, and the school mascot, which I still think should have been my horse Lucky.

Throughout my high school years, I made many good friends. I was somewhat of a passive kid. One might say I was shy. I didn't like conflict or trouble. I wasn't the popular kid, but I was liked by the teachers and I got along great with everyone – the smart kids, the jocks, and the hoods. That said, there was this one tough guy that picked on and bullied me for the first couple of months. One day when he was pushing me around, I grabbed him by his shirt, pinned him up against the wall, and let him know that I had had enough. He backed down after that day, and we became good friends and still are to this day. That was a good day.

I was the first person to break a bone at the new Franklin High School. I did it while playing football. The next year I went out for wrestling. In my prime, I was 6 feet 4 inches tall and weighed 180 pounds. Since then, my height has gone down and my weight has gone up. It must be a law of physics. That same year, while in study hall, the teacher left the room for some reason and a few of the kids started fooling around. They turned off the light, and since there were no windows in that room, it was pitch dark. One kid threw one of those big rubber erasers, hitting me in the eye. I put my hand to my eye and couldn't feel it. I was taken to and spent a week in the hospital. I was totally blind in that eye for about a month. My vision slowly came back and eventually recovered to near normal, but there is still some damage to this day. By this point, I had an A+ for the most serious injuries at the new Franklin High School. It was a school record and the best grade I received.

There were many good times during high school, and I have many fond memories of those years, but none of them involved schoolwork. A recurring theme of parent-teacher conferences was, "He's got more potential than this."

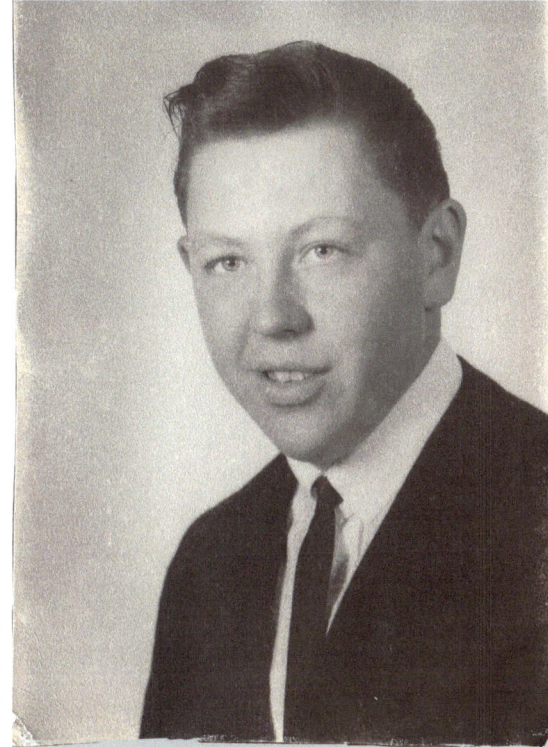

I failed two classes in high school. One was biology. Let's say it was because I had a crush on my extremely beautiful teacher and wanted to stay in her class. At least that's the story I'm sticking to. The other course I failed was Latin. I took the class because I wanted to go into the ministry. Because of this failure, I realized that I was not blessed with the abilities necessary for becoming a minister, since understanding Latin, Greek, Hebrew, and German was mandatory.

Thinking back to one day during my junior year, I know exactly where I was and what I was doing. Everybody my age does. I was in the hallway waiting to go into art class when it was announced that President John F. Kennedy had been shot by Lee Harvey Oswald. Everyone was in shock, and many were crying and uncertain of what was happening. It was a dark time in our history.

I often wish I was more scholarly, but book learning has never been one of my strong points. Most of my education came from learning things hands on in the school of life. I think my lack of scholarship was a big contributor to my lack of self-confidence and low self-esteem. However, I don't necessarily look at that as a negative. I've observed many people who have seemed overly confident with high self-esteem but have not impressed me nor achieved much in life, by my standards.

No, I was never a good student. Yet miraculously, I graduated from high school in four years with average to below average grades. Graduation from school was not the best day of my life, but it was definitely in the top 10.

POSTSCHOOL, PREMARRIAGE YEARS

The years after I finished school and before I met my future wife were what I would call my "wild" years. They were the days of teen bars, great music, fast muscle cars, and drag racing.

After I graduated, I got a full-time job at a machine shop. In addition to that job, l was a bouncer at a go-go bar at night. Now that I was making money, my first purchase was a palomino mare named Dixie and her buckskin colt Dixon. Dixie was a majestic horse – well-behaved yet spirited, and Dixon ran freely right alongside us, following his mother wherever we went.

Early the next year, I made a second big purchase – I bought my first new car, a 1966 Mercury Comet Cyclone. Three years later, I bought a 1969 Dodge Charger, one of the hottest cars at the time. The speedometer went up to 160 mph, but the fastest I got it to was only a little over 120 mph.

On weekends, my friends and I would go to Zivko's Ballroom, a teen bar and dance hall that was 50 miles from home. In those days, while drinking and driving was not a good thing, it was almost accepted by law enforcement. I remember my friends and I stopping on the side of the road to sleep it off, when a police officer stopped and told us we couldn't park there. He basically made us drive while intoxicated. It's amazing I came out of this period of my life alive. I knew some that didn't. It may sound strange when I say I was blessed to have a perforated stomach ulcer, but it truly was a blessing. It prevented me from drinking alcohol, and who knows where that might have led me.

Recreational drugs were around at that time, but I thank God that I never tried them. Don't get me wrong . . . I have and have had my own vices. I regrettably smoked cigarettes most of my life. I've also been intoxicated at times, mostly in my youth. Now I'll just have the occasional cocktail with family or friends. One thing I do have is a shot of brandy every morning, but I maintain that it is for medicinal purposes.

My postschool years were also the years when the Vietnam War was going on. Several of my classmates were killed in action. Those were not good times. I was up for the draft and went in for my physical, but I was rejected and unable to serve due to my perforated ulcer.

During this time, I took several trips to Canada to fish and hunt bear. One trip was with a group of older gentlemen from the area. When we arrived in Canada, we were supposed to have four Indian guides. We could only get two, and one of them we had to bail out of jail, but the fishing was fantastic. Another trip was with my cousin. Again, the fishing was fantastic, and I also shot a black bear.

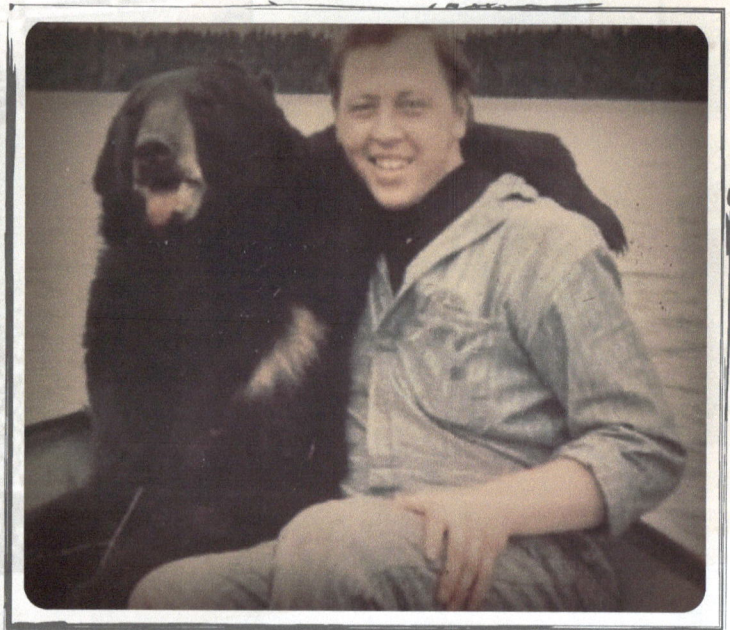

On July 20, 1969, a good friend and I watched the live, televised landing of Apollo 11 and the very first time man walked on the moon. The following week, he and I took a road trip, touring the west in my brand-new Dodge Charger. We visited many Western states and saw scenery that we had never seen before. We ended our trip in Las Vegas, where we attended various shows and concerts, including Elvis Presley and Petula Clark.

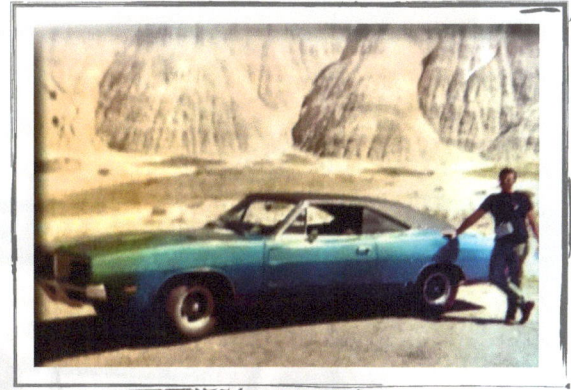

My passion for farming led to my next major purchases: a few registered Polled Hereford cows and a bull. Herefords were – and still are – my favorite breed of cattle, and their calves are the cutest. I rented and worked some land, raising mostly hay. I also raised oats, wheat, corn, and soybeans, depending on the year.

These were good years. They were free. I was an adult without the major responsibilities of marriage and children and the like. But the best was yet to come.

27

MY WORK LIFE

With school behind me, I decided to get a day job, even though my heart was in farming. My dream was to farm for a living, but it was only a dream and probably for the best that it didn't come true, which I'll explain later.

My Aunt Lorraine worked for Precision Screw Thread (PST) Corporation. It was a small, family-owned manufacturing company that did thread rolling, which is the cold forming of helical threads on metal parts. She arranged for a job interview for me, and the day of my interview was the day I met Glenn Simpson, the founder and owner of the company. Meeting him was a pivotal point in my life. At the time, I had no idea how influential the job and especially Glenn would be in my life. He was a devout Christian man with high moral and ethical standards, something that was important to both of us. He was also a very intelligent and honest man. I was hired that day with a starting wage of $1.75 per hour.

28

I started my employment at the original Greendale shop as a machine operator, operating a very dirty, smelly abrasive saw, cutting metal bars to length. Several months after I started, I woke up in extreme pain. The doctor came to our house, checked me over, and asked if I had eaten anything strange or had been out drinking the previous night. I explained to him that I hadn't. He said that if it continued, we should give him a call. By that afternoon, the pain was so bad that my mother called him back. The doctor told her to get me to the hospital. It took both my dad and my uncle Lyle to carry me out to the car.

At the hospital, while they were taking X-rays, I passed out on the table. They rushed me to emergency surgery at 8:00 p.m. that night. I woke up with a hose in my nose and a drainage line coming out of my stomach. When the doctor came in to see me the next morning, he told me I had a perforated ulcer and that the poisons from my stomach were draining into my body. He said I would have lived for only one more hour if they hadn't operated immediately. I remember asking the doctor how they got that drainage line in that was coming out of my stomach. He said, "Oh, that was easy; we just stabbed you there." I wasn't allowed to eat or drink anything for nearly a week. After that, I was allowed only a half-ounce of cream once an hour. On top of all that, I had recently placed an order for a 1965 Chevrolet Chevelle SS red convertible that now, due to the circumstances of the hospital stay and long recovery process, I had to cancel. My Grandma Blomberg happened to be in the same hospital at the same time I was. She had cancer and ended up dying while I was still there. I was unable to attend her funeral.

Shortly after I was able to return to work, I went on to operating thread rolling machines, then on to setting up these machines for others to operate, and then on to becoming the foreman. In the mid-1970s, we built a new shop in Muskego, Wisconsin.

I went into programming machines and engineering. I wasn't a degreed engineer, I was more of a practical, common-sense engineer. I was privileged to program computer numerical control (CNC) machines, design processes and tooling, and design and build machines and test stands.

Throughout my life and to this day, I have never had a lot of confidence in myself. Glenn kept trying to build my confidence, telling me there's a difference between educated and intelligent. I remember attending a vendor seminar with Glenn at IBM Corporation in Denver, Colorado. During a midmorning break, when we were having refreshments and talking with the other attendees, a man came up to me and asked me what company I was with and what I did there. I told him "Precision Screw Thread Corporation" and that I was an engineer but I didn't have an engineering degree – that I didn't go to college. He responded by saying, "Well, I didn't go to college either, and I'm the president of IBM." These things helped me considerably. I've learned that there are many highly educated people in our world – some very intelligent, some not so much, and even fewer that have wisdom. I still don't have a lot of confidence in myself. But maybe for me, that was a good thing.

We continued to grow as a company. We manufactured a large variety of threaded products from parts that went into manure spreaders, medical parts, and parts that went into outer space. We started leaning more toward the aerospace market and began manufacturing ball screw actuators. For instance, we manufactured the ball screws that operate the thrust reversers on jet engines. Soon, aerospace was half of our business. I became manufacturing manager and was in charge of all aspects of production. Glenn had previously made his son the president of our company, which continued for a number of years. He was an intelligent, educated engineer who was very creative and did many good things for us. Unfortunately, his skills did not extend to being a good president. Eventually, Glenn was forced to make the extremely difficult decision to let his son go. After it happened, Glenn and I went into his office and had a long talk about all that had happened and about the future.

Glenn then told me that he wanted me to be the president. My lack of confidence and my lack of experience with what's involved in being a president led me to tell him that I was honored but I wasn't sure if I was ready to be president. We decided that I would be vice president and he would take back the title of president, though he no longer wanted to be overly active. At a later time, the title "Vice President and Chief Operating Officer" was created for me.

Glenn and I did not have a traditional employer-employee relationship. We were, in his words, "confidants." He treated me like his own flesh and blood, and he included me in everything, even family meetings, which sometimes put me in an awkward position. He and I would sit in his or my office and talk about everything, from business to our faith. We even shared personal feelings about things. There were times when he would break down crying about his relationship with his son and the loss of his first wife many years prior. For many years my goal was to restore their father-son relationship. Eventually, I succeeded in helping to restore it and brought his son back to the company as a sales engineer. At the time, I viewed it as one of my biggest accomplishments.

Glenn and I both believed that our most valuable asset was the people – our employees and vendors. From the top down, we all considered ourselves to be the PST family. We took good care of them and they, in turn, took good care of the company. Company leaders are important, but they are not the ones that make companies thrive. We were blessed with a great group of people. Each had their own special talents. They were all different, all needed, and not one was more important than the other. They were the reason for our company's success. We had a profit-sharing program and a customer-service bonus program for the employees. We had company picnics, even beer parties after a good month. And every year, we had a Christmas party for all the employees, retirees, and their families.

Our largest event celebrated our 50th year in business. It was to be a formal, catered affair. We had a huge party tent installed and connected to the shop, and a band for evening dancing. All of our employees, vendors, customers, and their families were to be in attendance – even the Mayor of Muskego.

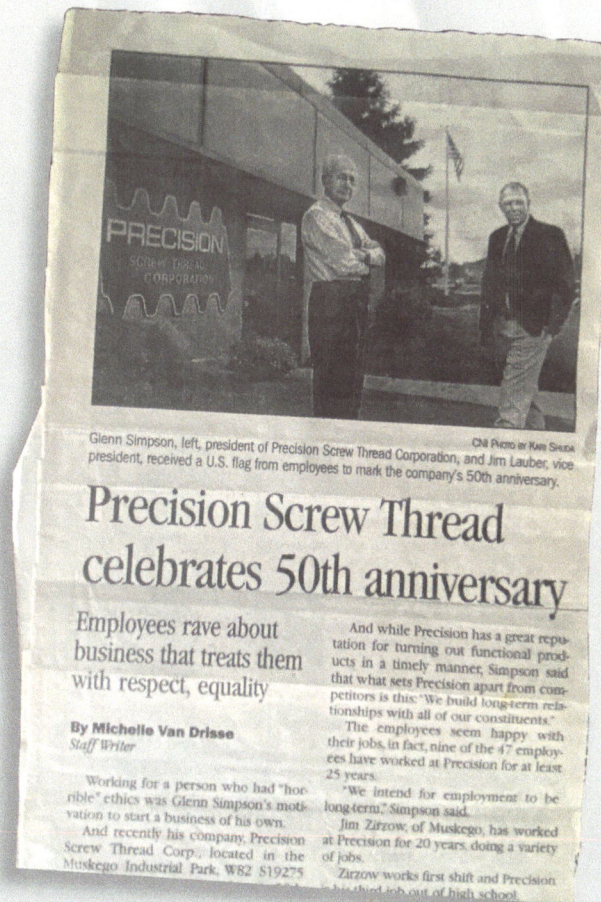

Glenn Simpson, left, president of Precision Screw Thread Corporation, and Jim Lauber, vice president, received a U.S. flag from employees to mark the company's 50th anniversary.

Precision Screw Thread celebrates 50th anniversary

Employees rave about business that treats them with respect, equality

By Michelle Van Drisse
Staff Writer

Working for a person who had "horrible" ethics was Glenn Simpson's motivation to start a business of his own.

And recently his company, Precision Screw Thread Corp., located in the Muskego Industrial Park, W82 S19275

And while Precision has a great reputation for turning out functional products in a timely manner, Simpson said that what sets Precision apart from competitors is this: "We build long-term relationships with all of our constituents."

The employees seem happy with their jobs, in fact, nine of the 47 employees have worked at Precision for at least 25 years.

"We intend for employment to be long-term," Simpson said.

Jim Zirzow, of Muskego, has worked at Precision for 20 years, doing a variety of jobs.

Zirzow works first shift and Precision his third job out of high school.

This is a portion of a newspaper article the Milwaukee Journal Sentinel printed the day of the celebration.

The employees had decided to take up a collection to purchase an American flag and flagpole that they were going to present as their gift to the company on the day of the celebration. Four days prior to the celebration, while listening to the radio on my way in to work, I heard about a plane crashing into the World Trade Center. As I got to the shop, there were more incidents, and we soon realized that we were under attack. That day 2,977 people were killed and more than 6,000 were injured. We were all in shock. The employees decided that there was no better time to present their gift to us, instead of on the day of the celebration. They asked Glenn and me to come outside where they were all gathered, and they presented their gift. I can't begin to describe the emotions of that moment, as all 50 members of our PST family stood in tearful silence as that flag was being raised. Not many people have the privilege of having a work family with so much love.

During the next several days, we deliberated about canceling the celebration because of the attacks. In the end, we decided to proceed and not let the terrorists win. The celebration went on, and it was an absolutely amazing day.

Over the next years, Glenn developed Alzheimer's. It was a long, slow progression that was difficult to watch because he was very aware of what was happening to him. Eventually, he was unable to come into work and was put into a nursing home.

With Glenn no longer being in control of the company, his sons saw the opportunity to take it in a new direction. Although it was not my plan to retire so soon, due to a difference in opinions, I was given no choice. After 46 years, I had to leave the job that I loved, as well as the employees, vendors, and customers I worked with, all of whom I considered dear friends.

My daughters decided that this was definitely something to celebrate, and they threw me a surprise retirement party with my relatives and friends and the entire PST family. From the speeches to the slideshow, I felt surrounded by so much love that day. Sadly, only six short years after my retirement, the company that we worked so hard to build had to be sold. However, the memories and friendships will last forever.

My job at PST was a great one, affording me a wide variety of experiences and exposing me to many people who had a positive influence on my life. It also allowed me to live the farm life through hobby farming. And if I hadn't worked at PST, I may never have met my wife, Judi. In the end, being forced into retirement turned out to be the best thing they could have done for me, giving me nine wonderful years of retirement to spend full-time with my wonderful wife before she died. God knew what I needed more than I did.

Judi and I continued to visit Glenn in the nursing home until he passed away. During my last visit with him, he was basically unresponsive. Before I left, I asked him if we could say a prayer together. I said the Lord's Prayer, and to my surprise, he mouthed every word with me. My last words to him were, "I'll see you in heaven."

FRIENDSHIP

*G*od has truly blessed me with many good friends throughout my life. Some have been lifelong and some are newer, but all have been good. For the sake of brevity, I have decided to pick just one – Dennis Kopecky – and explain how he became one of my best friends.

Dennis owned Eagle Grinding & Plating Inc., which did cylindrical grinding for our company. During the early years of our association, I quickly learned that Dennis was an honest man of great integrity, filled with fun, and he soon became someone I highly admired and respected. Over a number of years, we built a friendship that has continued to grow.

Every Christmas, he would bring Judi and me a turkey or ham and a bottle of Korbel. Eventually, he invited me to go deer hunting with him on a 30,000-acre ranch in Wyoming. Every year, he took a different customer or associate on this great adventure, so I knew this was a once-in-a-lifetime opportunity. It was also a dream come true for me. It was an amazing trip, and the ranch was beautiful. While I was there, I became friends with the rancher, his wife, and their family. And I did get a deer – actually, I got two deer. Dennis let me take a second deer on his license.

That was almost 25 years ago, and throughout those 25 years, our friendship has continued to grow. We've shared many good times, bad times, fun times, laughs, and tears together. We don't see or talk to each other every day, but we have built a rare friendship. I also had the pleasure of watching him and my wife Judi develop a special bond of their own. Dennis and Judi would kid around and joke with each other. He also gave her various pieces of the metal art that he created from old farm machinery – pieces that he and I would collect from the ranch we hunted on. This meant a lot to Judi and to me.

About four years ago, while Dennis and I were in the truck together driving home from our Wyoming hunting trip, he said, "There's something I never told you." He went on to tell me that after that first hunting trip so many years ago, he received a phone call from Judi telling him just how much I loved that hunting trip, and she asked him if he would continue taking me along. She then said, "But don't tell him I called you." That is the reason that I've been going on this "onetime," dream hunting trip for all these years. Even though Judi didn't enjoy me being gone, and spent one week every year being lonely, she selflessly arranged with Dennis for me to continue to go, solely for my happiness. And she never told me. That's true love and sacrifice. And what kind of a man changes his long-standing ritual just to accommodate me, all because of a phone call from a man's wife? God put both of these people into my life for a reason. What more does a man need in his life than a selfless and loving wife, a true best friend, and a loving God?

Dennis took Judi's fight with cancer and her death harder than anyone I know. Whenever we talked during her battle with cancer, he broke down in tears. Judi knew how he felt, and that made her feel so loved, which meant so much to me. At Judi's funeral, he cried like a baby and gave me a hug that I will never forget. My daughters already knew how he felt, but they witnessed his sincerity at Judi's funeral.

MY INTERESTS AND HOBBIES

Our lives are filled with so many things that we call "everyday life," and I was blessed with the time to enjoy some hobbies. Farming was perhaps my biggest. When I quit farming, trips to our cottage up north became our biggest hobby.

Fishing at our cottage in northern Wisconsin and fishing and bear hunting in Canada are also hobbies, along with deer hunting in both Wisconsin and in Wyoming on the 30,000-acre ranch.

Feeding the deer and other wildlife that frequent the land by the cottage is another. I went from raising cattle to having a small herd of deer. Judi and I never got tired of seeing them. They became our pets.

I enjoy photography – especially taking photographs of God's awesome creation with my mobile phone. I haven't yet upgraded to a good camera. God provides the scene; I just push the button.

After I retired, I began woodworking – designing and building everything from tree houses to furniture. Most of what I built was for our own use, but I also made things for others and gave them away. Selling them for profit would take the joy away.

I love throwing parties for family and friends, hosting people at our lake home, and making other people happy.

Taking care of the grandkids is another hobby. I call it a hobby because it isn't babysitting or something I have to do. It's a privilege to have mutual, loving companionship where I can relearn how to be young and innocent from them and they can hopefully garner some knowledge and wisdom from me.

MY LIFE WITH JUDI

Though every age of my life has been an amazing gift from God, this period, by far, was the most loving and fulfilling and made my life complete.

It all began when one of my employees set up a blind date for me – a date with his stepdaughter, Judi. At the time, I had no idea just how much I would owe this man for this one blind date that would change my life. We met at a bar that her mother worked at. When I first saw her, I felt something – I don't know if it was fear, butterflies, or awe. The date went well. We both had a good time, but I was afraid she was just being nice to me, that she didn't really like me. I didn't want her to think that I was overly anxious, and I guess I feared rejection, so I didn't call her for a week after that first date. During that week, her stepfather told me that she kept asking if I had said anything – if I liked her or if I thought she was pretty. I finally got up the nerve to call her. After that, we started dating. I try not to think about how I could have messed things up if I hadn't called her. I should have called her immediately the morning after that first date and told her how pretty I thought she was.

39

When I first met Judi, she and her sister Jan were living in an apartment with their mother. One day, shortly after we had started dating, Judi came home from work and found the apartment empty. Her mother had taken almost everything and moved to another state with her boyfriend, leaving Judi and Jan to fend for themselves.

Initially, I was only allowed to use the back door to their apartment. She didn't want me to see the names on the mailbox. She was either afraid, embarrassed, or ashamed for me to find out that she had been married previously. After a short time, she said she had something to tell me. We sat down, and she proceeded to tell me that she had been married before and that she had a daughter named Kimberlee Jean (born December 4, 1967). They were married when she was 18 years old. When things fell apart, he kicked her out of the house, and he and his family kept Kim and wouldn't let Judi see her. Judi didn't have any money or anyone to help her get Kim back. All of this didn't change my feelings for her. Together, we started a very important fight to get Kim back. I hired a lawyer, we went to court, and we won. Soon, Kim was back where she belonged.

From day one, I considered Kim to be my daughter and our first miracle. Judi's previous life was now history.

Throughout the next year, our love for each other continued to grow, and I decided that I wanted to ask her to marry me. We had already looked at rings at Robert Haack Diamonds in downtown Milwaukee. I went back and bought the one she had fallen in love with.

The night came when I wanted to propose. I made reservations at Dobie's Restaurant & Lounge in St. Francis, our favorite restaurant. I picked her up in my '69 Dodge Charger and off we went. She wore her best dress, one that we had picked out together. We got our table, and she ordered the lobster. Halfway through the meal, she bumped the butter warmer while dipping her lobster, and over it went, all over her beautiful dress. She was so embarrassed. After dinner, we went to Bradford Beach and walked down to the lakeshore. My plan was to romantically ask her to marry me under the moonlight, on the sand beach of Lake Michigan.

I was nervous and afraid that I might drop the ring in the sand. At just the right time and place, I started to ask her the most important question of our life, when all of a sudden, some drunk ran up and said, "Hey buddy, you got a church key?" Poof, there went that romantic moment. I just happened to have a bottle opener on my keychain. In an attempt to get him out of there as quickly as possible, I gave it to him and told him to keep it. He finally left, and I was able to recompose myself and proceed to ask her to marry me. She gave me the biggest gift of my life by saying yes. We couldn't wait to tell my mom and dad, so we immediately drove to the farm and got them out of bed. That was a good day.

In the following busy months, we had wedding plans to make. We went to Steinhafels and picked out all of our furniture and put it on layaway. I made monthly payments and had it paid off before we got married. My '69 Dodge Charger muscle car had to go, and we replaced it with a more appropriate family car. We took Bible information classes together, and Judi was confirmed in her faith one week before our wedding.

One month before we were married, we rented an apartment at the Wildwood Apartments on Wildwood Drive and Drexel Avenue in Oak Creek, Wisconsin. I moved in, while Judi and Kim stayed at her apartment until our wedding.

On May 6, 1972, we were married by Pastor Edwin Biebert at St. Paul's Lutheran Church in Franklin, Wisconsin. It was my home church – the same church my parents and grandparents were married in – and Judi and I were both now members.

Our wedding reception was held at the Wildwood on 76th Street, just south of Ryan Road. We had 325 guests at $1.75 a plate. The day after our wedding, my dad and I went to pay the bill. The owner/bartender was very friendly and thankful for our business. He kept buying us drinks – he would fill them up faster than we could drink them. We finally got out of there and went back to the farm. My dad said he needed to lay down for a minute, and out he went. I laid down and out I went. Judi, on her first day of married life, had to do the chores and feed the cows, because her new husband and father-in-law had to sleep one off. What a way to start a marriage! Judi just thought it was funny.

Judi and I had talked about what we wanted our life to be. She wanted a small house with a white picket fence, and she wanted to be a stay-at-home mom and raise our children, if we were so blessed. And we were. She also did in-home day care for many children over the years, all of whom benefited from Judi's care and influence in their lives. In addition, she took on an occasional part-time job at Gimbals for the Christmas season and a part-time job at Franklin High School when our children attended there.

42

We began our marriage living in the apartment that we had rented. This is where we had our second miracle, on February 2, 1973: Becky Lynn Lauber.

While we were still in this apartment, we bought our first puppy: a Keeshond we named Sheba. She was the best dog we ever had.

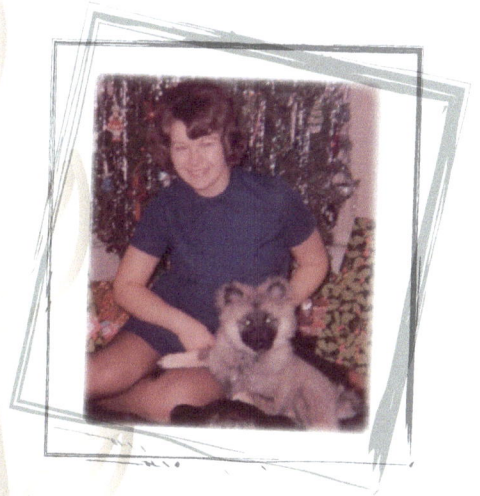

We then bought our first house – a 100-year-old farmhouse on South 76th Street in Franklin, Wisconsin. We were so proud and loved our new, old house.

The miracle in this house took place on August 22, 1976, when Jamie Syrena Lauber was born.

43

Just a little over a year after we bought this house, a developer wanted to build a subdivision around it and wanted to buy the back half-acre of our lot. We said, "No, but if you want to buy the entire place, we would consider it." They ended up buying the entire place. They were going to tear down the three-car garage, so I had them include it in the deal and had it moved to the Lauber family farm.

We then bought the farmhouse that was owned by my Aunt Lorraine and Uncle Lyle. They had just sold their farm and were moving to a farm in Berlin, Wisconsin.

This was a two-family house, so we were also now landlords. The miracle in this house happened on November 2, 1980, when Wendy Martha Lauber was born.

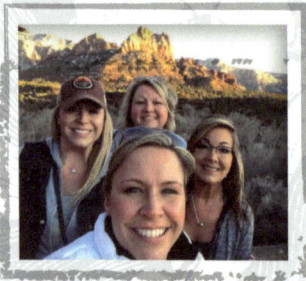

I almost decided to never buy another house, since up to this point in our marriage, we had a baby at each house we lived in! There are so, so many memories, stories, and accomplishments that I could write about all four of these amazing girls, our daughters, who are now successful grown women and great moms. Each one of them has brought so much joy and pride to our lives.

Judi always wanted to give me a son, but I didn't care what sex these precious blessings were, as long as they were healthy. I told her that my grandma always said, "If you have girls, the boys will come." And she was right – the boys did come. I can't imagine not having four daughters, and I have been so blessed having all girls. The only real problem was that we had only one small bathroom in a house with five females. At least I had a barn to pee in.

In 1981, we received the devastating news that my mother had stomach cancer and had only a few months to live. My dad dedicated his life to caring for her at home. Her doctor was later diagnosed with cancer, and he visited my mother at the farm to ask her how she was able to take the news and deal with dying so well. She was able to share her faith with him, at a time when he really needed it. He ended up dying before my mother did. She actually ended up living another two years after her diagnosis. She went home to heaven on her favorite holiday – Good Friday – between the hours of 12:00 p.m. and 3:00 p.m. My father lived for another five years and also went home to heaven during Holy Week. God works in mysterious ways.

Before they passed, my parents asked if Judi and I would buy the farm so that they wouldn't have to worry about money and so my dad would be taken care of after my mother was gone. So we decided to buy the farm. I remodeled the upstairs so that they would have a nice place to live, and Judi and I and our four girls moved in downstairs. We were back where I had started, and my girls were able to experience growing up on a small farm.

The first time I brought Judi to the farm, back when we were dating, she asked me where I kept the meat and potatoes that we fed the cows, and she thought there should be curtains on the barn windows. When we moved to the farm, Judi turned into the true definition of a city girl turned country. She embraced farm life, helping me wherever she could. Her favorite job was raking hay. She also drove the tractor, pulling the hay baler and wagon while I stacked the bales on the wagon. We had our own sign language for "slow down," "speed up," "more gas," and "stop." I loved when she would look back and smile at me – fond memories I will never forget. She helped unload hay, putting the bales on the hay elevator. She helped clean the barns and deliver baby calves and pigs. She would call me at work to tell me the cows got out; so I would come home, and together we would round them up.

I had a small herd of registered Polled Herefords. Later on, we added some Charolais and Chianina. At one point we had a total of 40 head, including the calves. That didn't last too long, since it required a lot of work and feed and I already had a full-time job. We grew corn, soybeans, wheat, and oats, which was also a lot of work. It's not that I didn't have help on the farm. I had Judi and the girls. I also had my sister Kathleen's children: Rusty, Brian, Julie, and Kurt. They were more like my own kids, rather than nieces and nephews. Brian went on to be my right-hand man throughout my farming years. I got him a job at PST, and he was always there to help me.

We decided that we would buy feeder cattle and feed them out. We bought our cattle at an auction barn in Lomira, Wisconsin. We would walk the holding pens to pick out the ones that we wanted to bid on, and then the auction would begin. One time, after I bought the cattle that we wanted to buy, two small Jersey calves were brought into the ring. Judi thought they were so cute and fell in love with them. I asked her if she wanted them. She smiled and nodded her head yes, so I gave her my number and told her to bid on them. She was very nervous – this was her first time bidding. She timidly nodded her head and raised her hand with each bid and then looked at me for my approval. The auctioneer finally said, "Sold to the lady with the number 42." She looked at me with that big Judi smile and her shrugged shoulders. She was so proud, and I was so proud of her.

We had horses and a pony for the girls, some sheep and pigs, and various fowl.

My favorite meals were the picnic lunches Judi would prepare and bring out into the field where I would be working. It was usually a BLT, chips, fruit, and an ice-cold soda. We would sit and eat together in the shade in God's beautiful creation.

Farm life with Judi was absolutely wonderful, but it was not always easy. We had to leave parties early because we had to do chores. There were times we had to put down animals because they were suffering. Machinery broke down, the weather sometimes didn't cooperate, and money was tight. Judi put up with all of it – she was such a selfless, hard-working person.

Once again, a developer was going to build a subdivision around our farm. We had only two-and-a-half acres and the buildings. I rented the farmland from various people in the area. The developer wouldn't give us what we wanted, so I split off a lot to build a new house for Judi. She deserved it after all the years she sacrificed for me and my love of farming. We then sold what remained of the farm to a private party, who then sold the back half to the developer.

That Christmas, our girls surprised us with a gift. As we opened it, we broke down in tears. It was a painting of the farm. They had hired an artist to paint the farm that we all loved. It's one of my most cherished possessions. I have it displayed on the wall over a shelf holding a rock from the barn's foundation, a wooden peg from the barn's beams, a slice from a pear tree on the farm, and a jar of the farm's soil.

The day they demolished the barn was a difficult day for all of us. It was a part of the entire Lauber family and who we were. To this day, farming is in my blood.

The house we had built on the lot I split off was a house that Judi and I fell in love with after visiting countless model homes.

We moved into our new house during a snowstorm in 1993. We only had a couple hundred feet to move, so with the help of my nephews and our girls, we were moved in by evening. We picked up a fish fry that night and had our first meal in our brand-new house.

With the high ceilings in this house, we were able to have a huge Christmas tree – more than 14 feet high – which I cut down in northern Wisconsin where I went deer hunting.

The farmer in me needed a barn, so I built one in the backyard.

In 2013 we sold that house, which sat on the last remaining piece of the Lauber family farm. The farm had been in our family for over a hundred years and was a beloved part of the Lauber family heritage.

We then bought a small condo, Unit G, at 8123 South Legend Drive in the city of Franklin, where we had lived all our life.

This was to be a place to sleep and hang our clothes when we came down from our retirement home to see the kids and grandkids. It ended up being much more, as we learned that we wanted to spend more time with family, and also during Judi's battle with cancer, which required frequent medical care in the Milwaukee area.

There were many good times and memories had in each and every house that we lived in. I've referred to these places as houses, but Judi always made sure that each one was a loving home.

Every year over Memorial Day weekend, Judi and I went up north to a cabin in Three Lakes, Wisconsin, with our closest friends Dick and Jayne Wolter (and no, they didn't have a dog named Spot). On one of those trips, I said, "We should buy a cabin of our own." My sister Kathleen and her husband Marty had always graciously let us vacation at their cottage in Neshkoro, Wisconsin. But we wanted something for our own. So, we took the day off from fishing and went looking at cottages. We found a lot for sale on the same lake we had been going to for many years. We ended up buying that lot in 1997, in partnership with Dick and Jayne. Dick wanted to wait five years before building, but after just months went by, I told him, "Life is short. I think we should build as soon as possible." One year later, we had a cottage built on it. It was an ideal situation with good friends, since neither of us was in a position to build on our own. We knew from the start that this would be a temporary situation. We had a big family, and we couldn't both retire there.

Judi and I continued to drive around looking at lake lots, with dreams of someday building our retirement home on one. In 2002, we saw a "For Sale" sign and drove down the driveway. We were disappointed when we saw that it wasn't an empty lot, where we could build our dream home, but instead had two old, small cottages on it. We were also confused as to which one was for sale. We drove to the realty office and picked up a brochure and found out that both cottages were one property. We returned two more times that day and absolutely fell in love with it, despite the fact that it wasn't what we were looking for. We returned home to Franklin and spent the following week talking about it, wondering if we could afford it. By the end of the week, I was on the phone making an offer. We ended up buying it, and it was one of the best decisions of our life.

My most precious memory, burned into my mind, was the day we closed on the property. After the closing, we returned to our new purchase. Judi and I were sitting on the deck, next to each other, in the two wooden lawn chairs that came with the property. We were all alone, looking out over the lake, taking in all the beauty of God's creation that surrounded our new cottage, when she turned and looked at me with her classic shrugged shoulders and that big Judi smile. I could feel her excitement, and I knew this was now her happy place. I will never forget the message she sent me with that expression on her face and the moment we shared.

In 2010 we were told it was a good time to remodel, because some of the restrictions had loosened. We started talking to Tom Gutbrod, who was the brother of Lee Gutbrod, a good friend of mine who worked for me and was my right-hand man at PST. Tom happened to be a builder in Three Lakes. We came up with the design together and began construction. Tom did everything he said he was going to do – a trait I highly admire. The rules said we had to leave two walls and the floor intact. Mysteriously, one of those walls fell over. And then the second wall fell over. What were the odds? Then Tom said, chainsaw in hand, "This is how we straighten the floor." Soon, the floor was gone too! The only part of the old cottage that we saved was the old, vintage fireplace.

Judi and I spent every weekend and every vacation day we had up there helping with construction, cleaning up, cutting trees, hauling brush to the dump – whatever needed to be done. One of Tom's subcontractors, after seeing what Judi and I were able to accomplish in a single weekend, asked Tom, "What are these people, nuts?"

During teardown, I found an inside wooden wall board with someone's name on it. I wished they had put a date on it so I could have known a little about the place's history. The next weekend when we came up, Tom had a pile of wall boards with names, dates, and information about where they were from. Apparently, it had been a resort at one time, and people had signed their name with a date and a message on the wall. The earliest dates were from around 1930. People had visited from all over the country. The farthest visitor was from Nome, Alaska.

Six months after the start of construction, we moved into our brand-new dream home.

Thanks to being forced into retirement, I was blessed with the privilege of spending nine wonderful years, full-time, with Judi, the love of my life, in our dream retirement home on the lake. All the family memories made in this place are priceless. My greatest satisfaction was just how happy it made Judi, especially in her last years of life.

We took many trips over the years, to Colorado, Louisiana, the Black Hills of South Dakota, Idaho, Yellowstone National Park, Las Vegas, Canada, Florida, Branson, Niagara Falls, San Diego, Paris, Spain, and Alaska.

Judi had always liked Panda bears, so I decided to secretly book a trip for us to California to visit the San Diego Zoo. I packed her bags, with our daughters' help, and prechecked them at the airport. I told her that I had to pick up some clients and we were taking them out for supper. We got to the airport and were waiting for their plane to land, when our daughters came around the corner to surprise her and see us off.

She was confused and asked, "What are you guys doing here?"

I said, "Honey, we're going to California to see the Panda bears."

She was shocked and asked, "What about picking up your clients Dieter and Rick?"

I said, "I made that all up to get you here."

She remarked, "But I don't have any clothes or makeup."

I told her, "Yes, you do. It's already packed and on the plane."

After all she had done for me, it felt so good to be able to do something special for her. Surprising her was one of those precious moments I will cherish in my heart forever, and she got to see her Panda bears. God had truly blessed our life together with so much love and goodness, and we were looking forward to so much more yet to come.

On January 19, 2018, Judi was diagnosed with pancreatic cancer. We knew from the start that there likely was no cure. Yet, we were hoping and praying for a miracle. She fought it for a year and a half, going through chemotherapy and its agonizing side effects. On January 29, 2019, during a hospital stay, we were told by her doctors that there was nothing more they could do for her. After the doctors left, we had our private time together with hugs, tears, and words. She told me, "You have to stay here, I'm going to a better place." Then she said, with a smile on her face, "I'm leaving behind quite a legacy." I called the girls and her sister Jan and told them to come to the hospital. When they arrived, I told them what we were told by the doctors. They each took turns having alone time with mom, to talk and share their tears with each other.

During the five months that followed, the girls and I spent as much quality time with her as possible. We went to see Phantom of the Opera in Milwaukee. We took a trip to Branson, Missouri, to the Sight and Sound Theater to see the show Samson. I took this photo of them all at a chapel in Branson.

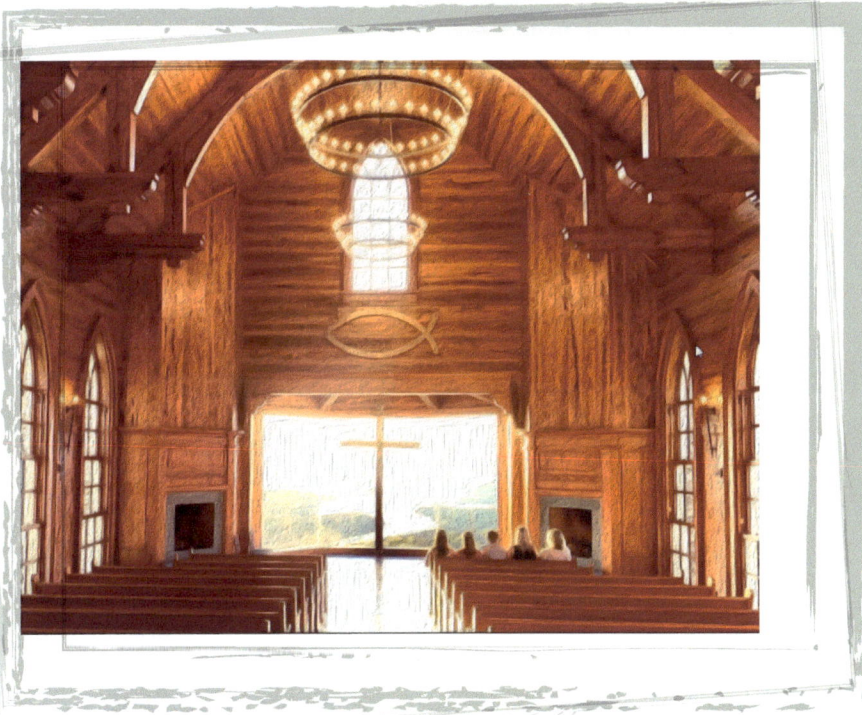

We celebrated her 70th birthday with the entire family.

We spent her final months up at our cottage – her happy place – where she wanted to be when she died. We celebrated our last wedding anniversary together there on May 6, 2019. A month before she died, we took her outside on the deck for some fresh air. Even with all she'd been through, and knowing she was near death, her classic sense of humor let me set her up with bottles of booze and a borrowed cigarette for a photo. I captioned it, "WHY NOT!"

On June 6, she stopped eating and went 17 days without food. Two weeks before she died, we took our last boat ride together.

Judi wanted to die in her happy place, but she also wanted to be with our children and grandchildren. Our selfless, loving daughters knew she wanted this, so they put their lives on hold and drove 500 miles round trip more times than I can count to spend every possible minute with their mom and me in her last days.

Judi's Happy Place

The week before she died, she said, "Are they going to do it in here? You should take everything off the walls." I realized she was thinking about being cremated. Then she asked me to take her wedding ring off, which I did. The week she died, she tried to tell me something. The only thing I could understand was "ing." I said, "Your ring?" She nodded yes, so I went and got her wedding ring and had the extreme honor of placing it back on her precious finger, just like I did 47 years before. Four days before she died, our daughter Becky put a wooden cross in her hand. She grasped it and held on to it tightly. I know she held it tightly because the day before she died, I tried pulling on it to see if it was just in her hand or if she was really holding on to it. She was holding on tightly.

On June 23rd, 2019, at her happy place, in the bed I built for her and under the quilt she bought in Branson, Missouri, Judi took her last breath and went home to be with Jesus, her Lord and Savior, with that cross in her hand.

Throughout this extremely difficult, year-and-a-half-long battle with cancer, never once did she complain or feel sorry for herself, nor did she show any fear. Her only concerns were for me, our daughters, and our grandchildren. I am in awe of the example she set for all of us, in her living and in dying.

After the girls returned home, I received phone calls from them telling me that they and the grandchildren were seeing rainbows all over the place. I was feeling left out, but as I turned and looked out over the lake, there was the biggest, brightest rainbow I had ever seen, and I knew she was home.

When I received her remains several days later, I decided to spend our last night together in her happy place. The next day, Judi and I made a long, final drive back to Franklin, with her belted in the passenger seat right next to me while listening to our favorite songs that were special to both of us.

On June 28, 2019, we had Judi's funeral at our home church, St. Paul's Lutheran Church in Franklin. The service was officiated by our son-in-law Pastor Chris Johnson. The readings were read by our brothers-in-law Pastor Tim Bauer and Pastor Tony Schultz. The music was played by our nephew's band Koiné. The first verse of "In Christ Alone" was sung by our 11 grandchildren. It was the most uplifting and comforting Christian funeral service I have ever witnessed. The outpouring of love for Judi, me, and our family by the 500+ people in attendance was humbling beyond words.

To my surprise, our home pastor had made a video of the service. This has become one of my most cherished and valued possessions. Though many tell me that I shouldn't watch and relive the grief, it brings me great comfort when I do.

Before Judi died, she told us, "If you ever see a crooked picture, that's me." Over the next several months, every time I turned around, there was another crooked picture.

Judi was the most loving and selfless wife, mother, grandma, and friend. She did everything possible to make me happy, from dressing to please me to shoveling manure so that I wouldn't have to.

As an example of her selflessness and our togetherness, she even went out in the woods with me, dressed in orange, and sat on a stump and did needlepoint while I was hunting deer a few hundred feet from her, just so we could be together.

She worked right beside me, no matter the task. We were both active at church: she sang in the choir and belonged to the Mary and Martha society, and I served on all the boards. Every decision throughout our life was talked about and made together. We never bought anything that we didn't both agree we needed and could afford. We did have a credit card, but we never carried a balance in all those years.

We didn't go out and spend money on entertainment or bars. We had each other, the greatest entertainment on earth. Going out for us was going to a wedding or visiting family or friends. We did absolutely everything together, outside of my annual deer-hunting trip. She was frugal – so much so that she washed and reused Ziploc bags. She could go into a store, buy four or five outfits off the clearance rack, and end up spending $16. Our grocery bills were nearly cut in half, thanks to her being the queen of couponing and buying smart. She did all the finances. She was also a cheap date: a glass of boxed wine, a box of Good & Plenty, a fire in the fireplace, and Wheel of Fortune on TV was a great night.

She put little love notes in the girls' lunch bags and was always there for them. She crocheted slippers, dishcloths, and blankets. She made the tastiest macaroni and cheese for the grandkids and was the best babysitter, taking them to the park and doing many other things too numerous to mention. She cared for our parents and her stepfather in their last days.

She was the best and most beautiful wife to me.

My life, since Judi went home to heaven, is not over, but I am less than half the man I used to be. My life has changed forever. I am so thankful for all of our awesome extended family and many close friends who are always there for me, and there are no words to express just how blessed I am to have all the love and attention I receive from our amazing daughters, sons-in-law, and grandchildren. They keep me busy and watch over me.

When Judi went to her heavenly home, it made me realize that our earthly life is short and my story here on earth isn't yet over. There were a couple of things that Judi and I always dreamed about doing, but we never got the chance to see them come true. Realizing I still have time, I decided to not wait any longer to make these things happen.

We had always dreamed of celebrating Christmas at the cottage with the entire family. A year and a half after Judi went home to heaven, I decided to make that dream come true and have a "Christmas for Grandma" up at our cottage for our girls, grandchildren, and Judi's sister. I cut down and put up a 20-foot Christmas tree for them to decorate when they arrived. It was an amazing celebration of Judi's life, with fireworks over the lake and all.

Next on my bucket list was skydiving. On my 74th birthday, I had the opportunity to jump out of a perfectly good airplane, 10,000 feet above my family waiting for me on the ground. Some may call that crazy, but I have always lived my life by faith. There is a reason that the words "do not fear" appear in the Bible so many times. Words can't describe my skydiving experience, but there's one thing I do know: I had never felt so close to God and Judi as I did during that experience. It was not just because I was thousands of feet above the ground, but it was because I was doing something I felt called to do. Although Judi wasn't there to witness Christmas or me skydiving, I know she would have smiled her big Judi smile at me.

I have no reason to be lonely, but I do miss her so very much, and I always will.

God has truly blessed me with this absolutely wonderful life. I've been asked, "If you could live your life over again, would you? And if you would, what would you change?" My answer to the first part of that question is "in the blink of an eye." The second part would not be to invest in more stocks or build a bigger, fancier house. While I did make mistakes and feel I could have lived life even better, there are very few things I would change.I pray that all those I love will be blessed to have a life as wonderful as I have had. It wasn't perfect – there were mistakes, disappointments, and failures. There were sicknesses, bumps, bruises, and broken bones. There was suffering and the grief of having lost loved ones. But I thank God for every minute of every age of my life and the people that He has put into it.

LIFE LESSONS

Life is a miraculous gift from God. I have learned many things throughout mine – some later than sooner – and I want to pass along just a few of them, that they might help you in your own. These things take effort, self-sacrifice, and faith, but the payoff will give you a true understanding of the phrase, "My cup runneth over."

- *Live within your means. Don't spend what you don't have, and avoid debt.*

- *Don't be afraid to make mistakes in life, as long as you learn from them.*

- *When you are interacting with people, always do what you said you were going to do. That's integrity.*

- *Remember that there is a difference between educated, intelligent, and wise. All three are good, but the greatest is wisdom.*

- *You are an example to someone, so be a good one.*

- *Surround yourself with good people – choose your spouse and friends wisely.*

- *Don't concentrate on doing the things that you think will make you happy. Instead, focus on making your spouse and others in your life happy. If you chose those people wisely, they in turn will bring more joy and happiness into your life than you could ever achieve by trying to please yourself. And don't just tell them that you love them. Tell them and show them, through your actions, just how much and why you love them.*

- *Make good choices. Always choose to do what is right and good, even when it's difficult. It's not about what life gives you, it's about what you do with what you've been given.*

- *Remember that life is all about God and people. Everything else is just stuff.*

- *Most important, keep God at the center of your life. Listen to Him through His Word, talk to Him in prayer, and share Him with others.*

This is the day the Lord has made,
let us rejoice and be glad in it

Psalm 118:24 – The Lauber Family Verse

www.ingramcontent.com/pod-product-compliance
Lightning Source LLC
Chambersburg PA
CBHW042011090426

42811CB00015B/1611